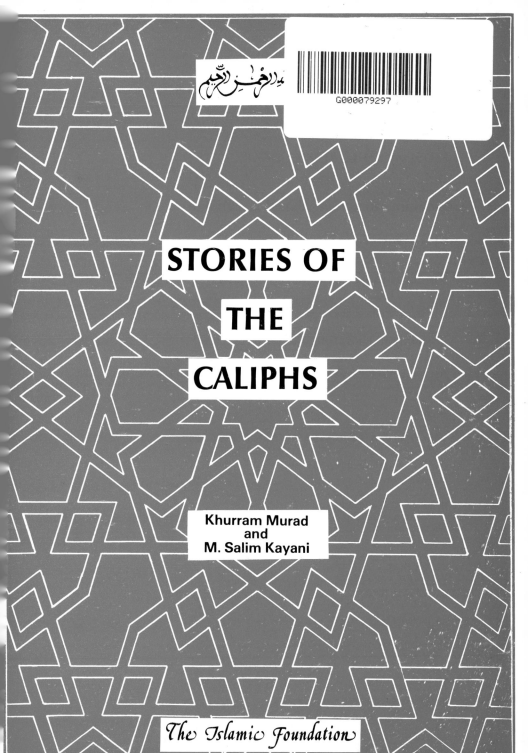

بِسْمِ اللهِ الرَّحْمٰنِ الرَّحِيمِ

STORIES OF
THE
CALIPHS

Khurram Murad
and
M. Salim Kayani

The Islamic Foundation

© The Islamic Foundation 1982/1402 H   Reprinted 1985, 1989 and 1996.

ISBN 0 86037 116 6

MUSLIM CHILDREN'S LIBRARY

General Editors:
Khurram Murad and Ahmad von Denffer

STORIES OF THE CALIPHS

Writers and researchers:
Khurram Murad and M. Salim Kayani

Illustrations: **Foqia**

Editors: **M. Tarantino and T. Greig**

These stories are about the Prophet and his Companions and, though woven around authentic ahadith, should be regarded only as stories.

Published by:
The Islamic Foundation, Markfield Dawah Centre,
Ratby Lane, Markfield, Leicester LE67 9RN, United Kingdom

Quran House, P.O. Box 30611,
Nairobi, Kenya

P.M.B. 3193, Kano, Nigeria

British Library Cataloguing in Publication Data
Murad, Khurram
        Stories of Caliphs. —— (Muslim children's library; 8)
        1. Caliphs —— Juvenile literature
        2. Arabia —— History —— Juvenile literature
        I. Title   II. Series
        953'.02'0922   DS236
        ISBN 0 86037 116 6

Set in 14/16pt Oracle

Printed by:
JOSEPH A. BALL (Printers) LTD., Leicester

MUSLIM CHILDREN'S LIBRARY

An Introduction

Here is a new series of books, but with a difference, for children of all ages. Published by the Islamic Foundation, the Muslim Children's Library has been produced to provide young people with something they cannot perhaps find anywhere else.

Most of today's children's books aim only to entertain and inform or to teach some necessary skills, but not to develop the inner and moral resources. Entertainment and skills by themselves impart nothing of value to life unless a child is also helped to discover deeper meaning in himself and the world around him. Yet there is no place in them for God, who alone gives meaning to life and the universe, nor for the divine guidance brought by His prophets, following which can alone ensure an integrated development of the total personality.

Such books, in fact, rob young people of access to true knowledge. They give them no unchanging standards of right and wrong, nor any incentives to live by what is right and refrain from what is wrong. The result is that all too often the young enter adult life in a state of social alienation and bewilderment, unable to cope with the seemingly unlimited choices of the world around them. The situation is especially devastating for the Muslim child as he may grow up cut off from his culture and values.

The Muslim Children's Library aspires to remedy this deficiency by showing children the deeper meaning of life and the world around them; by pointing them along paths leading to an integrated development of all aspects of their personality; by helping to give them the capacity to cope with the complexities of their world, both personal and social; by opening vistas into a world extending far beyond this life; and, to a Muslim child especially, by providing a fresh and strong faith, a dynamic commitment, an indelible sense of identity, a throbbing yearning and an urge to struggle, all rooted in Islam.

3

The books aim to help a child anchor his development on the rock of divine guidance, and to understand himself and relate to himself and others in just and meaningful ways. They relate directly to his soul and intellect, to his emotions and imagination, to his motives and desires, to his anxieties and hopes — indeed, to every aspect of his fragile, but potentially rich personality. At the same time it is recognised that for a book to hold a child's attention, he must enjoy reading it; it should therefore arouse his curiosity and entertain him as well. The style, the language, the illustrations and the production of the books are all geared to this goal. They provide moral education, but not through sermons or ethical abstractions.

Although these books are based entirely on Islamic teachings and the vast Muslim heritage, they should be of equal interest and value to all children, whatever their country or creed; for Islam is a universal religion, the natural path.

Adults, too, may find much of use in them. In particular, Muslim parents and teachers will find that they provide what they have for so long been so badly needing. The books will include texts on the Quran, the Sunnah and other basic sources and teachings of Islam, as well as history, stories and anecdotes for supplementary reading. Each book will cater for a particular age group, classified into: pre-school, 5-8 years, 8-11, 11-14 and 14-17.

We invite parents and teachers to use these books in homes and classrooms, at breakfast tables and bedside and encourage children to derive maximum benefit from them. At the same time their greatly valued observations and suggestions are highly welcome.

To the young reader we say: you hold in your hands books which may be entirely different from those you have been reading till now, but we sincerely hope you will enjoy them; try, through these books, to understand yourself, your life, your experiences and the universe around you. They will open before your eyes new paths and models in life that you will be curious to explore and find exciting and rewarding to follow. May God be with you forever.

And may He bless with His mercy and acceptance our humble contribution to the urgent and gigantic task of producing books for a new generation of people, a task which we have undertaken in all humility and hope.

M. Manazir Ahsan
Director General

4

contents

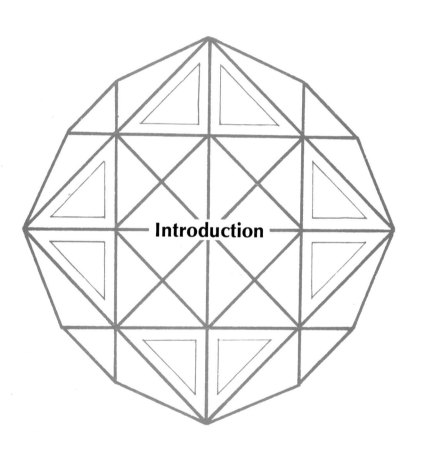

Introduction

Before the Prophet Muhammad (Peace and Blessings be upon him)* died, he was successful in bringing all of Arabia, from one end to another, under the rule of one God. No person was master of another; all were equal before their God – He alone was their Master, to Him alone did they submit. To govern justly and kindly according to the law of God and to care for people were as much acts of worship as to pray, to fast and to perform Pilgrimage; this was what the Blessed Prophet taught and practised.

After he died, his followers chose Abu Bakr to lead them and rule over them. He was called 'Khalifa Rasul Allah,' which means 'successor to the Messenger of God.' They called him 'Khalifa' or Caliph as he was not only a successor of the Blessed Prophet in government but he was also bound to lead the people on the path to Allah in accordance with His guidance and the traditions and examples given by the Blessed Prophet. For Caliph also means 'agent' or 'viceroy.' They also called him 'Amirul Muminin,' which means 'the ruler of the Believers.'

After Abu Bakr, Umar, Uthman and Ali were elected Caliphs – all were true followers of the Blessed Prophet and closely observed his example. There were many other Caliphs after them who were called Caliphs, but not all of them followed in the footsteps of the Blessed Prophet. Many lived luxuriously, did not act justly, oppressed people and denied them their rights, did not alleviate their misery and poverty and used public money for their own comfort.

* Muslims are required to invoke Allah's blessings and peace upon the Prophet whenever his name is mentioned.

However, those who did follow the Blessed Prophet left glorious examples for others to follow.

These were honest men. They lived simply. They ate and dressed like ordinary people. They were just and kind. They dedicated themselves to serving their brothers and sisters, and their fellow citizens, and thus they served their God. Even their governors and civil servants conducted themselves as nobly as did the Caliphs.

The Caliph is the most important person in a Muslim state, but he is not the sovereign. Nor are the people. God only is sovereign. No Caliph, nor even the entire Muslim nation, can make any law which is against the law of God, nor can any Caliph be obeyed, against His law. The Caliph is the head of state, the spiritual leader of Muslims. He has the enormous responsibility to see that:

> The people live according to God's will, in peace and happiness. They do not live in hunger, unsheltered, uneducated and uncared for.
>
> Good prospers and evil is weakened.
>
> Justice is done in all manners and matters and oppression is put down.
>
> Public money in the government treasury is spent for the welfare of the people.
>
> Law and order are maintained throughout the land.
>
> The penalties as decreed by God for serious social crimes are fully carried out.

You can see from this list what an important job a Caliph has.

Because the Caliphs were successors to the Blessed Prophet, they looked after their people as a father would his children. This involved doing three things. Firstly they set a good example in their own lives and showed others how to live properly. They never used their office nor the treasury for their own ends. Secondly, they were very particular in taking good care of the poor and needy. And thirdly, they treated all as equals, the mighty and the weak, the high and the low, the rich and the poor.

Here are some stories about the early Caliphs.

How the Prophet lived

One day Umar came to the Prophet's (Peace and Blessings be upon him) house to see him. The Blessed Prophet lived in a small apartment which bordered his mosque. These apartments are now included in the beautifully-built Mosque of the Prophet in Madina. But at that time the walls were built of mud and stones, the roof of palm leaves and stalks and the floors of sand. The doors gave onto the courtyard and hall of prayer.

Umar came to the door and sought permission to enter. 'May Umar bin al-Khattab enter, O Prophet of God?' said Umar.
'Yes, come in, Umar,' the Blessed Prophet replied.

Umar entered the room where the Blessed Prophet was resting. He first greeted the Blessed Prophet 'Peace be with you.'
'And with you be peace,' replied the Blessed Prophet.

Umar sat down on the floor and began to notice the room for the first time. There was no bed in the room. The Blessed Prophet was lying on a mat. Part of his body was on the floor and part on the mat. The mat was rough and the floor hard. The marks from the mat were visible on his body. He was wearing a garment of rough and coarse cloth. He had a pillow, but the pillow was filled with prickly leaves from a palm tree. There was nothing else in the room, no wardrobe, no rich food to eat, no comfortable mattresses. Instead, in a corner were some berry leaves and a small heap of barley, over which an untreated piece of leather was hanging.

Tears began to well up in Umar's eyes. When the

Blessed Prophet saw Umar crying he asked him, 'Why! What are you crying about, Umar?'

Umar answered in a bitter voice, 'And why shouldn't I cry, O Prophet of God? I see your bedding and the marks from the mat on your back; I see all your belongings which amount to nothing, and yet you are the Prophet of God and His chosen Messenger! The emperors of the Byzantine and the Persian empires are living in luxury and comfort. Their thrones are made of gold and their clothing and bedding are made of the finest silks'. Umar waved his arm to illustrate. 'And this is all you have – this is your treasure.'

The Blessed Prophet smiled and looked kindly and affectionately at Umar. 'Are you not happy, O Umar that we shall receive our riches and treasures and comforts in the eternal life. The kings of this world have received their full share here, and even this share is going to be useless for them as soon as they depart from this world. Our share is to come later, but once we receive it it will remain with us forever.'

Umar understood then that the government the Blessed Prophet was going to establish was not a government of kings and emperors but a government of the servants of Allah who live not for this world and its transient rewards and comforts, but for the world to come, for the everlasting rewards and treasures to be found in the Hereafter.

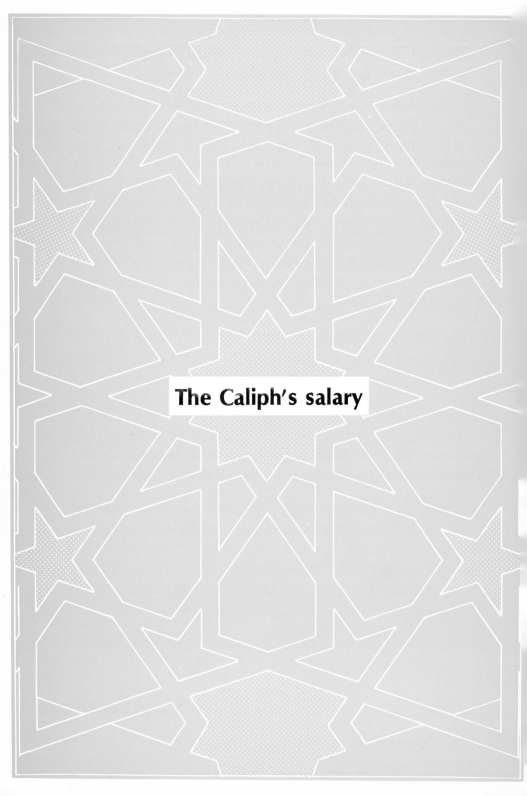

The Caliph's salary

As you know, Abu Bakr was the first Caliph to be elected by Muslims to rule over them and manage their affairs.

Early the next morning after his election, Abu Bakr appeared in the market-place. All his life he had been a merchant who sold cloth, so as usual he was still trying to be a merchant even though he had been named Caliph and ruler of Arabia. People were sorely puzzled when they saw him arrive loaded down with rolls of cloth on his shoulders. But they just didn't know what to do about it.

Finally, when Umar appeared, he immediately went up to Abu Bakr and said 'What are you doing with all this cloth?'

'I am going to the bazaar,' said Abu Bakr.

'What for?' asked Umar. 'You have now to manage and run the affairs of the entire Muslim community. How can you find time to carry on business?'

'But I have to earn my livelihood,' replied Abu Bakr. 'Otherwise how shall I feed my family?'

Umar thought for a moment. Then he said, 'We have to find a way of solving this problem. Obviously you cannot find time to continue selling cloth. Come with me and let us go and consult other Muslim brothers.'

Umar went with Abu Bakr to see Abu 'Ubayda. He was in charge of the treasury. He was also declared by the Prophet (Peace and Blessings be upon him) to be the most trustworthy and honest person in the whole Muslim community. Other responsible leaders of the community were called in for consultation. Umar

Caliph's Salary

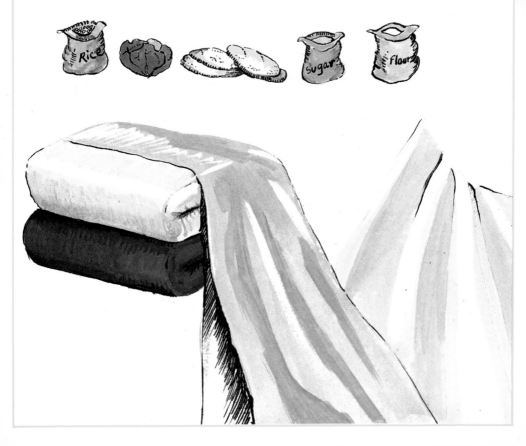

proposed that a salary should be fixed for Abu Bakr to be paid out of the public treasury and which would take care of his needs. But how much? That was the question. Abu 'Ubayda proposed 'Abu Bakr should be given a salary equivalent to what is needed by an ordinary lower middle-class man to sustain himself.'

After some discussion the first Caliph's salary was fixed as follows: he would be allotted two sheets of cloth in summer and two sheets of cloth in winter. In addition he would be given food for himself and his family for every day.

Abu Bakr happily accepted this allowance. But at the same time he deposited every penny that he had of his own in the public treasury. It was not necessary, but he insisted on doing so because he did not consider it honest to keep his own wealth while the treasury was taking care of his needs.

Abu Bakr gave up his business for his Muslim brothers wanted him to do so. He and his family continued to live on the small grant which the Muslims had given him. The money was only just enough to support his family and he had only a modest standard of living. But he lived contentedly and in peace and happiness.

One day his wife came to him and said 'I wish we could afford to buy some sugar. I want to make some sweets for you.'

'Dear wife,' replied Abu Bakr, 'I am afraid we have no money. You could go to the Baitul Mal (the public treasury) for some but the money in the public treasury belongs to the people; it has to be used for their welfare and for the state. It would not be right for us to take any more than what has been fixed as our salary.'

His wife graciously accepted what Abu Bakr said but she still wanted to make him some sweets. So every day she saved a little something from the money she had for housekeeping. After a few days, she had enough money to buy some sugar and make some sweets, which she did.

'How did you manage to buy sugar to make sweets?' said Abu Bakr when he saw the sweets at dinner.

His wife replied 'I saved a little money each day from the housekeeping. That is where I got the money from.'

'I am amazed,' said Abu Bakr. 'Although you have saved money every day to buy sugar, we still seem to have eaten well. This shows that we have been taking more money from the treasury than we really need.' Abu Bakr then reduced even further his own very small grant from the government, and he and his wife lived off that smaller grant for the rest of their lives.

Around two years later when Abu Bakr was about to die, he called all his children to his bedside. 'I would like to know the total sum of what I have used from the treasury' said Abu Bakr. The children made calculations and told him the exact amount that he had drawn from the public treasury.

'When I am dead, sell my property and deposit whatever I have in the Baitul Mal so that every penny has been replaced' said Abu Bakr.

By this final and conclusive decision, he left nothing in his will but repaid all that he had received from the State during his lifetime.

When Umar, who was elected to fill the vacancy caused by the death of Abu Bakr, was informed of Abu Bakr's last decision, he simply wept. 'O Abu Bakr, you have set an example which those who come after you will find almost impossible to follow.'

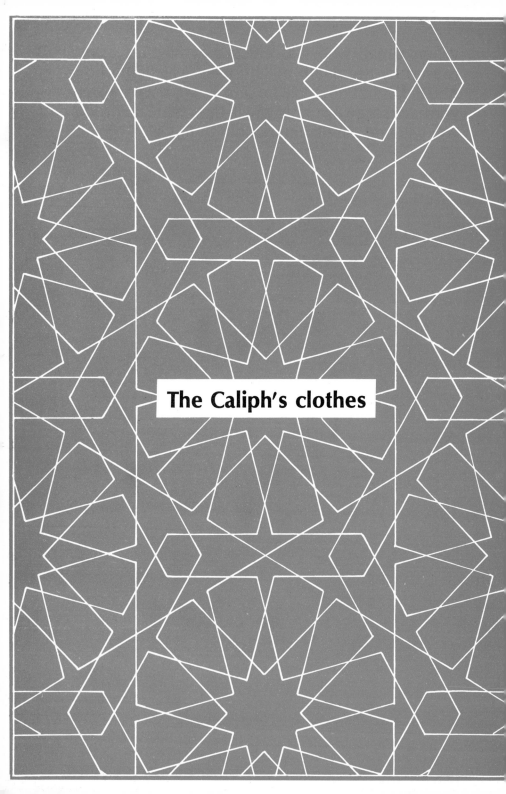

The Caliph's clothes

Umar, who was the second Caliph, received the same salary as Abu Bakr. He used to dress simply and eat frugally. He used to wear old clothes, which had patches and were threadbare. His shoes often had holes in them. He often had nothing to eat but barley bread and olive oil.

And yet, under him, the Islamic government extended as far and as wide as Iran, Iraq, Syria, Egypt and even North Africa. The Roman and Iranian empires crumbled and their riches and treasures flowed into Madina.

Umar was a wise, just and popular Caliph. He had many friends who loved him because he was such a good man. But even so, his friends could not understand why he dressed so badly and ate so poorly. 'It is not right,' they used to say. 'Don't you see how he dresses and how he lives. We Muslims have entered Iran and Iraq. We now rule over fertile lands. We have wealth and riches. There is no need for our Caliph to go around in old clothes and have almost nothing to eat. Kings and princes and ambassadors and deputations come here from many lands and mighty empires and they wear tunics of the finest silk. Why cannot our Caliph be like them? Umar has just got to say the word and our tailors will make him the finest clothes in the world. And our cooks will cook the finest foods which will be brought to him in the morning and in the evening.'

One day an ambassador of the Roman Empire came to Madina. He wanted to obtain an audience with Umar. He was used to palaces and kings. So he asked people in the streets 'Where does your king live?'

'We have no king' said the Muslims to whom he had put the question.

'But you have someone who is the head of your government?' asked the bewildered ambassador.

'Yes, we have appointed one from amongst us who looks after the affairs of state. If you go straight up this road you might find him somewhere.'

The Roman ambassador went up the road to which he was directed. Finally he found Umar resting under the shade of a tree wearing two garments, one of which had twelve patches.

Finally, people could not take it any longer. Knowing that Umar was facing extreme hardship, they assembled and began discussing the matter.

'I think we should propose to Umar that his salary be increased so that he may dress more appropriately, thereby making a better impression on visiting ambassadors and deputations. Also he would be able to buy and prepare good food for himself as well as for others who come to visit him,' said Zubair, one of the close followers of the Prophet (Peace and Blessings be upon him).

'I fully agree with you. I was also thinking along the same lines,' said Ali.

Believing that Ali would be the most suitable man to talk to Umar about this matter they asked Ali to place the matter before him. But Ali said 'I certainly do not dare go to Umar and talk to him about this.'

So 'Uthman came forward with a suggestion. 'We all know how Umar is. He will hardly like the idea of taking more from the treasury. Let us first somehow find out how he will take the proposal. Let us go to Hafsa his daughter and seek her help.' All those present agreed with 'Uthman's suggestion, and so they went to find Hafsa.

Now, Hafsa had also been one of the wives of the Blessed Prophet. For this reason, they felt that Hafsa could persuade her father to give up wearing old clothes, or at least she could find out how he would react to their proposal. Hafsa listened to them and said, 'I agree with you. But even I do not find the courage to go to him and talk about this matter. I want to help you but let us seek the help of 'Aisha.'

'Aisha was the daughter of Abu Bakr and had also been one of the wives of the Blessed Prophet. Umar greatly respected her. They found her in agreement with their proposal as she also realised the hardships which Umar was facing. 'I shall go to Umar and have a word with him and find out how he feels about this proposal' said 'Aisha.

'I don't think he will ever agree,' added Hafsa, 'but at least we shall know.'

'Don't tell him who we are' they requested as they left.

The next day 'Aisha and Hafsa went to Umar. Hafsa, seeing her father sitting there in clothes which were old and patched, shook her head and sighed.

'Aisha said to Umar, 'O chief of Muslims, do I have permission to talk to you about a certain matter?'

'Yes, with great pleasure, O mother of Muslims' said Umar.

'Aisha chose her words carefully. 'Allah has blessed you with the conquest of the treasures and cities of Heraclius, the emperor of Byzantium, and Chosroes, the emperor of Persia. Ambassadors from important foreign powers and deputations from within Arabia come to visit you, and stay with you. And you are wearing a cloak which has twelve patches. If only you would wear fine, handsome clothing and serve more succulent meals, you would make a better impression on those who visit you.'

'Father,' said Hafsa. 'Please forgive me for interrupting but I have a serious question to ask you.'

'Please ask your question, my child,' replied Umar.

'Dear father, what I want to know is this,' she said. 'Why ever do you wear such old clothes? Why do you go about with clothes which are patched and threadbare? When people come to the Caliph they expect to see someone dressed like a Caliph. And what is more, you don't seem to notice that you are wearing old clothes!'

For a while Umar kept silent. 'Aisha and Hafsa thought that the Caliph must surely be angry. Then tears began to well up in Umar's eyes. He wiped away the tears with his sleeve and then smiled sadly. He knew how much courage it took for 'Aisha and his daughter to speak out to him like this. For a long while he said nothing. Then he looked at them carefully and said to them, 'You were the wives of the Prophet. If anyone knows how he lived, you do.'

Then he turned to 'Aisha, 'Tell us O mother of Muslims, did the Prophet ever eat wheat bread for three days running? Was his stomach ever full? Or did he ever have complete meals both in the morning and in the evening?'

'No' said 'Aisha, 'not till the day he died.'

'And you know, 'Aisha, that the Prophet had a cloak without a lining which he used to put on in the daytime and on which he used to sleep at night?' said Umar.

'Yes,' said 'Aisha.

Umar continued. 'And there was a mat in his house on which the Prophet used to sit in the daytime and when night came he used to sleep on the same mat?'

'Aisha could not contradict him. 'Yes, you are right, Umar.'

And then Umar turned to Hafsa. 'Tell me, when the Prophet went to sleep, what did he use for a bed? Didn't you tell me, Hafsa, something like this: "I had a mat in my room. When the Prophet wanted to go to sleep I used to spread the mat out on the floor. So he would lie down on that mat. But the mat was rough and the floor hard. Very often he woke up with the marks from the mat on his back. In fact I felt he did not sleep at all well on the mat." And didn't you, Hafsa, also tell me: "One night I folded the mat over double to make it more comfortable for him to sleep on. And that night the Prophet slept so well, in fact, that he did not get up for the pre-dawn Prayer. Only when Bilal called the Azan did he wake up. As soon as he woke up he asked me, 'O Hafsa, what did you do with the mat last night?' When I told him, he asked me not to fold the mat over double again. He wanted to sleep on the mat as it was before."

'And don't you know, Hafsa, that all the Prophet's errors were forgiven. Still he used to be hungry when evening came and used to stand and bow and prostrate himself before Allah for long hours during the night.

'You have both been the wife of the Prophet. You both are the mothers of Muslims,' said Umar to 'Aisha and Hafsa. 'Have you come to me in order to lead me to the comforts of this world, to give up the rewards of the Hereafter? The only example I would like to follow is the example of my two friends, Muhammad and Abu Bakr. I know I wear old clothes and I know my friends all talk about me for doing so. My clothes are uncomfortable and look awful. So is my food which many do not want to share with me. But I also know that the Prophet and Abu Bakr lived a very simple life and cared little for their own comfort.

'So answer me this question. When the Prophet lived like this caring so little for his own comfort, how can we his followers want to live in luxury? And can't you see I do this for the love of the Prophet and Allah?

'And finally, will you tell me who sent you to me with this proposal?' asked Umar.

'This I cannot tell you', said Hafsa. But neither Aisha nor Hafsa could say a single word. Nor could any of the Caliph's friends who were told of what Umar has said.

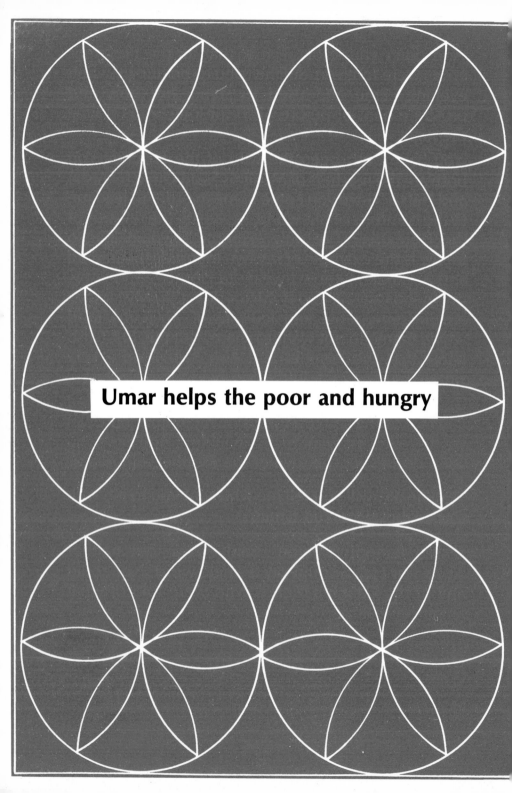

Umar helps the poor and hungry

Umar was the second Caliph. He succeeded Abu Bakr. Umar was hard working and conscientious because he was a true servant of God. A Caliph should take care of the Muslims in his state as a father takes care of his children. Umar tried his very best to do this. In the daytime he used to work at home. At night he often went out into the city of Madina to help any of his people who were in need.

One night Umar was walking down a street in the city when he heard some children crying. The crying came from a small house. When Umar looked in, he saw a lady sitting with her children around her. The lady looked very sad and the children seemed to be very hungry.

Umar noticed that there was a pot on the fire. He thought that there must be some food in the pot and that soon the lady would give it to the children and then they would stop crying. Umar watched and waited while the contents of the pot kept boiling away but still the lady did not feed the children. In the end he wondered what was the matter.

Finally, Umar went into the house and asked the lady why her children were crying. She told him they were crying because they were hungry. 'Isn't the food in the pot ready yet?' he asked.

The lady came close to Umar and whispered in his ear, 'Do not tell the children. There is no food in the pot, because I do not have any money to buy food. The pot has only water in it but the children think that there is some food in there. They are hungry now but if I wait long enough, they will cry themselves to sleep. Then they will forget their hunger.'

When the children finally dropped off to sleep, the lady explained to Umar that her husband had just died. That was why she had no money to buy food. Unfortunately the people in charge of the Baitul Mal did not know of the lady's trouble. If they had known, they would have helped her.

Then, Umar, who was sorry for the poor woman, said to her, 'Why ever did you not tell the Caliph about this?'

'I am a woman,' answered the lady, 'I cannot go about looking for the Caliph to tell him my troubles. If he is really the Caliph, he should know about them. It is his duty to help people in trouble. I feel our Caliph is not doing his duty properly. Umar has let me down. I don't think he ought to be Caliph if this is how he treats his fellows who are in need.'

Umar was shocked when he heard what the lady said. He ran to the Baitul Mal and put some flour, meat and sugar in a bag. As he was going to take it back to the lady, one of his servants stopped him and offered to carry the bag for him. 'I shall carry the bag myself,' said Umar. 'On the Day of Judgement you will not be able to carry my burdens for me, so there is no reason why you should carry them today.'

The Caliph carried the bag of food to the lady's house. When he got there, he himself cooked the food for the children, and it was he who fed them. As he was leaving the house, the lady said to him 'You should be Caliph, not Umar. You are kind, generous and understanding. That is what a Caliph should be like.'

'Lady,' replied the Caliph, 'I am Umar. It was wrong of me not to know of your trouble. But now your children have been fed and are sleeping happily. I have also arranged that from today on, the Baitul Mal will give you a grant so that you will be able to support them properly until they grow up.'

The Caliph's feast

Umar bin 'Abdul 'Aziz was another Caliph who feared God and followed the example of the Prophet (Peace and Blessings be upon him). He was called Umar the Second. Many of his predecessors had not been good rulers, but he lived a simple life, even though he ruled over vast territories from the Atlantic Ocean in the West to the River Indus in the East. Before he became Caliph, he also lived luxuriously like all members of his family, the 'Ummayads, who ruled over the Muslims after Ali. But as soon as he assumed the Caliphate he gave up all luxuries. He restored justice and rule of law. He confiscated all the wealth and lands illegally acquired by the members of his ruling family and returned them to either the treasury or to the rightful owners. Every day he worked hard and tried to show others by his own efforts how to live properly.

Many of his officials followed his example. Although they were important people, they also lived good, simple lives. Some officials, however, took little notice of what the Caliph said or did. Among these was Bismallah, who was head of the Muslim army. Bismallah was an excellent soldier. He was a brave and fearless man whom all the soldiers loved and respected. But he had one weakness – he was much too fond of good food. He used to spend at least a thousand dirhams a day on food for himself alone.

When Umar came to hear about this, he was unhappy. He thought about the poor and the needy. A thousand dirhams a day could provide an awful lot of food for those who had none. Because Umar was the Caliph, he felt he had to do something about his friend's greed, but it was difficult to know how to go about it.

He thought long and carefully about the problem. Suddenly, he had an idea.

Umar sent a servant to Bismallah and invited him to lunch the next day. He then summoned his cook and said to him: 'Tomorrow I want you to prepare the finest lunch you have ever made. I leave it to you to decide what to cook. I have invited Bismallah to come and eat. Prepare whatever you think will really please him. And when you have done all that, cook a bowl of porridge as well.' The cook thought the Caliph had taken leave of his senses, but he did as he was told.

Bismallah looked forward to dining with the Caliph. In fact by the time he arrived at the Caliph's house he was already very hungry. The Caliph received him kindly and began asking questions about the army. How were the soldiers doing? Where were they training? Had the officers in the army enough men? And so on and so forth. The more the Caliph talked, the hungrier Bismallah became. Of course, he could not let the Caliph know how hungry he was – that would not have been polite – but he felt the pangs of hunger all the same.

The Caliph knew anyway how Bismallah felt. He could tell by the look on Bismallah's face that he was absolutely starving. Suddenly Umar stopped asking questions and called for the cook. The cook came quickly. He was expecting the Caliph to ask him to bring in the huge meal which he had so carefully prepared. The Caliph looked at the cook and said with a smile, 'Bismallah is getting hungry. Bring him a little something to keep him going until lunch time. Bring in the food I asked you to prepare last of all.'

The cook, dismayed by this request, came back with the bowl of porridge which he placed before the Caliph who offered it to Bismallah, who was so hungry that he immediately started to gobble it down. When Bismallah had finished eating the porridge, Umar asked him a few more questions. Then he called for his cook again and asked him to bring in the lunch.

The cook was delighted; he had worked very hard to prepare such a splendid meal. Bismallah just loved roast peacock, curried lamb, saffron rice, honey cakes and sweet meats. But Bismallah took one look at the food and said 'I'm afraid I cannot eat another mouthful. I am full up after eating the bowl of porridge.'

When Umar heard this, he said, 'My dear friend, the oats for this porridge did not cost more than one dirham. Tell me, if you can eat well for one dirham, why do you spend more than one thousand dirhams a day buying food for yourself alone? Allah does not like spendthrifts. If you spent those thousand dirhams on the poor and needy, Allah would love you more.'

Bismallah was so impressed by what the Caliph said that from that day on he spent much more of his money on helping the poor than on feeding himself.

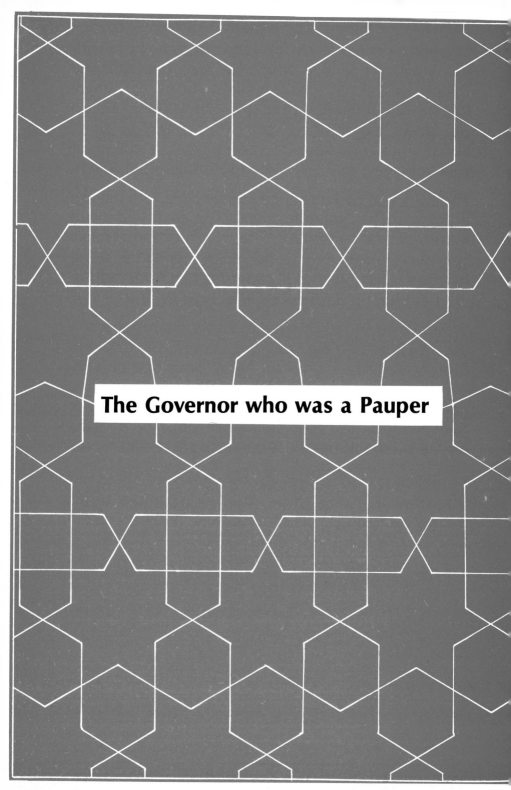

The Governor who was a Pauper

In the days when Umar was Caliph, he was presented with a problem which he found very difficult to solve. After considerable thought, he summoned his friend and colleague Sa'eed bin Amir to his side. 'Sa'eed,' said Umar, 'I just don't know what to do. The people of Homs have come to me for the fifth time complaining about their governor. I have tried to accommodate them by appointing men whom I thought were suitable, but apparently each one turned out to be a disappointment in one way or another. There just isn't anyone left to whom I can entrust such a position. Except,' he added, 'for one who happens to be facing me at this moment. And so,' continued Umar with a smile, 'I hereby appoint you Governor of Homs.'

Sa'eed was completely taken aback. He knew the people of Homs were difficult to accommodate. Sa'eed felt he was in no way qualified to govern anyone, let alone the people of Homs. He shook his head unhappily. 'Umar,' he said, 'by Allah I plead with you not to place such a trial before me. I could never undertake such a position.'

'What,' exclaimed Umar suddenly losing his temper, 'you helped saddle me with the responsibility of the Caliphate, and now you won't help me carry out that responsibility? I won't stand for it, Sa'eed. You will just have to accept this appointment whether you want to or not. This is an order I am giving you.'

Sa'eed had no other option but to obey Umar. After he had settled his affairs in Madina he reluctantly came to say goodbye to Umar.

'Now brother,' said Umar appeased, 'don't look so

distressed. I am convinced that with Allah's help you will be able to handle the job perfectly well. Now, one last matter. Let us decide on your salary.'

Sa'eed looked surprised. 'What do I need with a salary? What I receive from the treasury is more than enough.'

Umar laughed. 'Allah be with you, Sa'eed' he said, and to show that he was well pleased, embraced him and sent him on his way.

Off went Sa'eed to Homs, and for some time Umar heard nothing from that part of the world. Umar was relieved. 'Things must finally be going smoothly,' he said to himself, 'I was right in appointing Sa'eed.'

One day a delegation from the people of Homs turned up at Umar's house as was customary several times a year. Umar asked them for news of their district and they replied to Umar's satisfaction. Finally, Umar asked to be shown a list of the poor and destitute, that they could be given funds from the general treasury. The list was given to Umar who checked it over and frowned.

'Who is this Sa'eed bin Amir? Can there be two such people with the same name?' he asked.

'Certainly not,' replied the delegate. 'That is Sa'eed bin Amir, our governor.'

'What, you write his name down here as if he were a pauper?'

'But he is a pauper, respected brother,' replied the other with arms outstretched, 'he's the poorest among us. Days pass when you'll not smell cooking from his stove, I warrant you.'

Umar dropped his head, and when he raised it again, the visitors noticed his beard was damp with tears. 'We shall take care of this' said Umar softly, and invited the delegation to retire.

When the delegation headed home the next day, they were carrying one thousand sovereigns from the Caliph Umar to be given to Sa'eed bin Amir, Governor of Homs. Once back at Homs, the delegation proudly presented the gift to Sa'eed in a sheepskin purse. Sa'eed thanked them warmly, but when they had left and he discovered what the purse contained, his face paled, and he dropped the purse as if it were a curse. 'From God we come and to God we return,' he murmured as one does when faced with death.

His wife, overhearing him, was shocked. 'Oh what has happened?' she exclaimed. 'Who is dead? Did the Amirul Muminin die?'

'Worse than that,' answered Sa'eed.

'Worse than that? What could be worse, dear husband?'

'What would you say if something came to lure me away from the everlasting life? What would you say if corruption entered our house?'

'Why, get rid of it' cried his wife, 'flee from it.'

'And will you help me do that? asked Sa'eed of his wife.

'With pleasure, husband' she replied.

So by the end of the day, the thousand sovereigns which Umar had given Sa'eed were distributed amongst the poor of the regions of Homs.

It wasn't long after that that Umar, who was making his regular visit around the provinces, stopped at Homs. As soon as he arrived the inhabitants gathered around and began complaining again about their governor. Umar was astounded and dismayed. 'How do you expect me to believe you this time?' he scolded. 'Five times in succession I have replaced a governor in Homs, and recently I have sent you the best man I have, a faithful and true servant of Islam and still you dare to complain. This time I insist that Sa'eed bin Amir be present in person to defend himself against your charges, and you will soon see, ungrateful lot that you are, how mistaken you must be.'

With this said, Umar marched off to his quarters. But in his heart he wondered secretly how Sa'eed could have displeased these people, and he prayed to Allah that his good opinion and faith in Sa'eed be not shaken. The next morning, everyone, including Sa'eed the governor, assembled at Umar's quarters. 'Now,' announced Umar in a loud voice, 'may the first man who wishes to voice a complaint against your governor come forward.'

From out of the crowd stepped a young man, robust and strong, who was evidently not afraid to speak his opinions before the Caliph.

'Oh leader of the faithful,' he began, 'the fact is that our governor is lazy. He does not come out of his house until late in the morning.'

'Not only that,' interrupted another standing in the crowd, 'but on some days we don't even see him until evening. Who knows what he does all day long in his house.'

Umar winced at these accusations, and turning to Sa'eed, asked:

'What is your explanation for this conduct?'

Sa'eed shook his head. 'Allah is witness that what I am about to confess is both distasteful and embarrassing to me. The fact is that I have no servant to help me. So, early in the morning, I knead the dough, and then I bake bread. Following that I perform my ablutions. Then I come out to meet the people. But since I only have one change of clothes, sometimes I am also obliged to wash them, and wait for them to dry; sometimes I have to mend them, before venturing out of my house.'

Now, no one suspected that Sa'eed had no servant. In those days everyone of importance had a servant, and certainly a governor would have more than one. This fact shed a different light on the accusations, and Umar's faith in his friend was restored.

'Any more complaints?' called out Umar.

'Yes, I have one,' grumbled an old man. 'We older citizens like to gather in the evenings and talk about the past, but Sa'eed here is unfriendly and never wants to join us.'

Umar turned again to Sa'eed for an explanation.

'Well, the fact is, that I would rather keep vigil all night and worship Allah than to talk idly of past glories,' confessed Sa'eed.

Umar smiled broadly at Sa'eed, and called again to

the crowd: 'Are there any more complaints against this man who is your governor?'

'Well, yes there is,' cried a merchant. 'When he does join us, he quite often seems to be thinking of other things, and once he even fainted before our very eyes for no particular reason!'

At these words, Sa'eed's face turned dark and he bowed his head for a moment. Umar waited for his friend to speak. Finally, Sa'eed began to explain in a low voice. 'I have not always been a Muslim, as you know. There was a time when I was an idolator, and that period of my life is always horrible for me to remember. The time I passed out, I was remembering when Khubaid bin Ady was being tortured to death... I was there, and I watched as they cut his body into pieces, and he not yet dead! (here, Sa'eed shielded his eyes with his hand and began to sob). I did nothing to stop them.... I just stood there... and then when they asked him if he would prefer Muhammad to be in his place, he replied "Never. A thousand times will I accept death rather than allow even a thorn to prick Muhammad's side." Ah! when I remember that I did not lift a finger to help this saintly man, my self-disgust overwhelms me, and I feel as if God will never forgive me.'

A long silence followed this confession. Umar, touched by the story and proud of his friend, exclaimed 'Praise be to God! Sa'eed is indeed a true servant of God, and my faith in him is justified.'

Umar then sent another thousand sovereigns to Sa'eed in order to ease his situation. When his wife saw the money she was delighted. 'Praise be to God!'

she exclaimed. 'Now we will be able to hire a servant to help us with the housework and have something left over for ourselves.'

'Dear wife,' said Sa'eed, stroking his wife's head gently, 'shall I tell you what would be even better than that?'

'What would be better than that?' asked his wife.

'We shall give it to someone who will give it back at a time when we might be in even greater need than now.'

'And how will that be?'

'We shall give it as a loan to Allah' said Sa'eed. 'For if we do so, then you may be sure it will return to us many times over.'

His wife agreed, and in no time at all the whole amount had again been distributed to the poor of Homs.

Such were the natures of the men who ruled over the Islamic countries in the early days.